To Simone Kaplan—
To Life!
—L.B.H.

To Linda Kjome & Roy Staub
with love, and with awe,
and with respect
—L.S.

Acknowledgments for permission to reprint poems
in this collection are found on p. 32.

Lives: Poems About Famous Americans
Text copyright © 1999 by Lee Bennett Hopkins
Illustrations copyright © 1999 by Leslie Staub
Manufactured in China. All rights reserved.
For information address HarperCollins Children's
Books, a division of HarperCollins Publishers,
10 East 53rd Street, New York, NY 10022.
http://www.harperchildrens.com

Library of Congress Cataloging-in-Publication Data
Lives : poems about famous Americans / selected by
Lee Bennett Hopkins ; illustrated by Leslie Staub.
     p.   cm.
   Summary: A collection of poetic portraits of sixteen
famous Americans from Paul Revere to Neil Armstrong,
by such authors as Jane Yolen, Nikki Grimes, and X. J.
Kennedy.
   ISBN 0-06-027767-X. — ISBN 0-06-027768-8 (lib. bdg.)
   1. United States—Biography—Juvenile poetry.
2. Children's poetry, American.   [1. United States—
Biography—Poetry.   2. American Poetry—Collections.]
I. Hopkins, Lee Bennett.   II. Staub, Leslie, 1957–   ill.
PS595.B48L58   1999   98-29851
811.008'3520313—dc21   CIP
                                                    AC

Typography by Carla Weise
09 10 11 12 13 SCP 10 9
❖

LIVES

Poems About Famous Americans

Selected by
Lee Bennett Hopkins

Illustrated by
Leslie Staub

HarperCollins*Publishers*

CONTENTS

INTRODUCTION

Through fourteen poems, twelve especially commissioned for this collection, moments in the lives of sixteen caring, daring, sharing individuals who shaped and changed the course of American history are highlighted.

Each poet brings a distinctive personality to life, focusing on goals, aspirations, struggles, and the influence these icons have had on society.

Men and women in the fields of science, history, sports, art, and literature who left an indelible mark on the entire world are depicted in a wide range of poetic forms—rhyme, narrative, and free verse.

The power of poetry! Power that makes us appreciate the magnitude of lives filled with courage, enthusiasm, inspiration—lives that have sparked hope and will provide role models for generations to come.

Lee Bennett Hopkins

THIS BELL RINGS FOR LIBERTY

Lawrence Schimel

On Fish Street lay my father's shop
    where metals bent beneath the blows
    of hammers falling fast as rain.
I learned the craft of smithing there.

The sparks now dancing 'cross the anvil
    shaping silver to form a bell
    remind me of his steady hand
so near the furnace blazing bright,

and of that night when my hands shook
    with fear upon the reins. We ran.
    Her steel-shod hooves falling hard
against the stony streets struck sparks.

We raced against the British troops,
    their coats as red as heated ore;
    we raced to warn militiamen
that soldiers landed on our shore.

The hammer's heavy head recalls
    my mind to the work at hand.
    That day is long behind us now
though much remains still to be done.

I quench the heated metal shell
    and fiery red begins to fade,
    the way we drove Redcoats to sea
and quenched them from our homes and land.

Paul Revere
1735–1818

A SONG FOR SACAGAWEA
Lewis & Clark Expedition—1803–1806

Jane Yolen

There were forty-five before her:
frontiersmen, good hunters,
stout, healthy, unmarried,
accustomed to the woods;
watermen, robust sailors;
experts on botany, carpentry,
forestry, smithery,
navigation by the stars.
One was master of the universal Indian signs,
one a black slave named York.
They carried powder and balls,
pork, purgatives, Peruvian bark,
beads for the natives,
writing desks and "creyons,"
six papers of ink powder,
a swivel gun with bullets,
casks of gunpowder,
a Newfoundland dog.

They knew how to read
words on a page
points on a map.
But they could not read the rest:
how broad the mountain-hemmed plains
how deep the winter chill,
how wide the river fords,
how far good faith could travel.
They did not speak
with the tongue of the Shoshone,
they did not know
the Hidatsa words for peace, for war.

She spoke for them,
helped them passage through
   the rough divides.
She dug roots for them,
wild artichokes,
when all they had to eat was parched corn.
She put up the tent,
packed it down again,
her infant son in a cradleboard on her back.

Was she a hero?
Did she get a medal?
Was she counted an explorer
who charted the way?
These are notions of the white man.
She was a Shoshone woman,
slave to the Hidatsa,
won by a French trader in a bet.
Carrying her son on her back,
she did all the white men did,
all that had to be done
to keep them alive on the long trail.
She was Sacagawea.

It was enough.

Sacagawea
1787?–1812?

ABE
Alice Schertle

And so,
young Abe
    of the too-short pants
    and too-long legs,
young Abe spitting into his palms,
wrapping his bony fingers around
    the handle of an axe,
sinking the bright blade deep
    into heartwood,
young Abe splitting the rails apart

grew into Abe
    of the sad eyes
    of the face carved deep
    by sorrow,
wrapping his strong hands
    around a nation,
trying to hold the bleeding halves
together

until they healed.

Abraham Lincoln
1809–1865

WALT WHITMAN
David Bouchard

He said that he would leave us
To go searching for his fancy
On the open road—the dark brown path
We all will come to know . . .

No matter if he was a man
A woman or a falling star
A *kiss* was left for us to share
A song was left to understand
A message sung through life then death
That *he* dared dream aloud . . .

Walt Whitman
1819–1892

THE WHIPPOORWILL CALLS

Beverly McLoughland

No one hears her
Coming
Through the woods
At night
For she is like
A whippoorwill
Moving through the trees
On silent wings.

No one sees her
Hiding
In the woods
By day
For she is like
A whippoorwill
Blending into leaves
On the forest floor.

And one night
The whippoorwill calls
And the warm air
Carries the haunting sound
Across the fields
And into the small dark cabins.

And only the slaves know
It is Harriet.

Harriet Tubman
1820–1913

AMERICAN WIZARD

Lawrence Schimel

A shout
rang out
in Menlo Park
one New Year's Eve

as people
stepped down
from the train
into dark

and he pulled
the switch—

a flood of light
lit up the night!

What marvelous lamps
without gas
or flame!

The people cheered
Thomas Edison's name
and his marvel
that turned dusk
into
day.

Thomas Alva Edison
1847–1931

TILL
Tom Robert Shields

No roses seen.
No songbird heard.
No moonlight.
Not a single word.

Till . . .
      Annie
          came.

Then—
Words,
Sudden, near.
Pulsing,
Clear.

Then—
Moonlight, roses, bird.
Word-wings
Felt, heart full, heard.

Not moon.
Not bird.
Not song.
Not word.

Till . . .
      Annie
          came.

Anne Sullivan Macy
1866–1936
Helen Adams Keller
1880–1968

ELEANOR ROOSEVELT
Rebecca Kai Dotlich

She chiseled out
the rarest place;
First Lady of the World, that face—
a portrait
of beguiling grace
endeared her to us all.

Who among us can't recall
the words she spoke
to soothe the poor.
And soldiers who had been to war
declared her *their own*
Eleanor.

Our First Lady Eleanor;
this Nation's charming chancellor.

Anna Eleanor Roosevelt—
No one knows the burdens *she* felt,
and yet,
her gentle spirit stirred
a passion in
the land she served.

She calmed the crowds
each time she spoke.

Her gallant words
helped those to cope
who hadn't dared,
before,
to hope.
Courageous deeds so humbly dealt—

We miss our Mrs. Roosevelt.

Eleanor Roosevelt
1884–1962

WHEN BABE RUTH HIT HIS LAST HOME RUN

Louis Phillips

When Babe Ruth
Hit his last home run,
It was as if the sun
Had set
Upon some huge continent
Called baseball.
After all,
Nothing Ruth did
Was small.

60 home runs
in '27.
No one had ever done
That before.

And still, after so many years,
Deep
In our sleep,
We want to be like him.
Run bases like him,
Be in the movies
Like him,
Be larger than life
Like him.

O, Babe, come back
Hit one more
Homer
For one of your earth's children.

George Herman "Babe"
Ruth
1895–1948

DREAMER

Lee Bennett Hopkins

He let us kiss
the April rain.

He shared his
hope
and
pride
and
pain.

He wrote
of life
with an ebon pen
and the world
was never
the same
again.

He syncopated beats
of Harlem-blues.

O!
The might
of
Langston Hughes

"Bring me all your dreams,"
he said.

And though
he died . . .

*He
is
not
dead.*

Langston Hughes
1902–1967

THE MANY AND THE FEW

For Rosa Parks, Part-time Seamstress
Montgomery, Alabama, December 1, 1955

J. Patrick Lewis

It was an Alabama day
For the Many and the Few.
There wasn't really much to do;
No one had very much to say

Until a bus, the 4:15,
Drove by. But no one chanced to see
It stop to pick up history.
The doors closed slowly on a scene:

The quiet seamstress paid her fare
And took the one seat she could find,
And, as it happened, just behind
The Many People sitting there.

The Many People paid no mind
Until the driver, J. P. Blake,
Told the Few of *them* to take
The deeper seats. But she declined.

Blake stopped the bus and called police;
And Many a fire was set that night,
And Many a head turned ghostly white
Because she dared disturb the peace.

To celebrate the ride that marks
The debt the Many owe the Few,
One day of freedom grew into
The Century of Rosa Parks.

Rosa Lee Parks
1913–

JFK: PERSEVERANCE FURTHERS
Nikki Grimes

There goes that famous flash
   of teeth—
a toothpaste model's dream.
But yours was not a model's
   smile.
(Few things are what they
   seem.)

Those pearly whites were good
   for more
than boyish charm's display.
The men of PT 109
discovered that the day

Your vessel sunk and you
   found strength
to tow a man to shore,
his life-vest strap clamped
   'tween your teeth
for five hours' swim or more.

Old injuries inflamed your
   spine.
The pain, you held at bay.
But then again, you never gave
adversity full sway.

Not family tragedy, nor death
nor ills, oft and abrupt
could cheat you of your goals
   except
to briefly interrupt.

In time, lest anyone forget,
you made this nation proud,
rekindling freedom's dream,
and denouncing bigotry out
   loud.

You brought us to the brink
   of war,
and to the edge of space.
You boldly took what risk
   seemed right.
That, time cannot erase.

No matter how much history
is stretched, or changed,
   or bent,
the fact remains that you
   were both
Hero and President.

John Fitzgerald Kennedy
1917–1963

MARTIN LUTHER KING DAY
X. J. Kennedy

Solemn bells in steeples sing:

Doctor
Martin
Luther
King.

He lived his life
He dreamed his dream:
The worst-off people
To redeem,

He dreamed a world
Where people stood
Not separate, but
In brotherhood.

Now ten-ton bells together swing:

Remember
Martin
Luther
King.

•Martin Luther King, Jr.•
1929–1968

FIRST MEN ON THE MOON

"The Eagle has landed!"
Apollo 11 Commander Neil A. Armstrong

"A magnificent desolation!"
Air Force Colonel Edwin E. "Buzz" Aldrin, Jr.

July 20, 1969

J. Patrick Lewis

That afternoon in mid-July,
Two pilgrims watched from distant space
The Moon ballooning in the sky.
They rose to meet it face-to-face.

Their spidery spaceship *Eagle* dropped
Down gently on the lunar sand.
And when the module's engines stopped,
Cold silence fell across the land.

The first man down the ladder, Neil,
Spoke words that we remember now—
"Small step for man . . ." It made us feel
As if we too were there somehow.

Then Neil planted the flag and Buzz
Collected lunar rocks and dust.
They hopped like kangaroos because
Of gravity. Or wanderlust.

A quarter million miles away,
One small blue planet watched in awe.
And no one who was there that day
Will soon forget the Moon they saw.

Neil Alden Armstrong
1930–
Edwin Eugene "Buzz" Aldrin, Jr.
1930–

NOTES ON THE LIVES

PAUL REVERE: Born on Fish Street, near the edge of Boston Harbor in Massachusetts, Revere worked in his father's silversmith shop from the time he was fifteen years old and remained an artisan throughout his life. On April 18, 1775, he rode from Lexington to Concord, Massachusetts, on horseback, warning patriot leaders that British troops were about to invade the area. This became known as "The Midnight Ride" and marked the start of the American Revolution. Henry Wadsworth Longfellow's "Paul Revere's Ride," one of the most popular poems in American literature, was inspired by Revere's bravery.

SACAGAWEA: An important figure in nineteenth century American history, Sacagawea, a Native American Shoshone, has had more memorials dedicated to her than any other American woman. In 1803, President Thomas Jefferson ordered Meriwether Lewis and William Clark to find a route from St. Louis, Missouri, to the Pacific Ocean. Two years later in a village on the Missouri River, the team met Sacagawea, then a teenager, who joined the excursion and became an invaluable guide and interpreter. She was able to identify important landmarks remembered from her early childhood years, find much-needed natural foods, and determine whether tribes they would meet were friendly or hostile by examining moccasin tracks. Due to her courage, determination, and resourcefulness, she was praised in the journals recorded by Lewis and Clark.

ABRAHAM LINCOLN: America's sixteenth president is one of the most revered men of all to have served our country. He had little formal education and worked at various jobs including rail splitter, ferryboat captain, and clerk in a general store before becoming one of the most successful trial lawyers in Illinois. In 1861, when he took office as president, the nation was in a tumult over slavery and states' rights. This conflict led to the Civil War, a devastating four-year battle between the Northern and Southern states. Lincoln's life is told in *Lincoln: A Photobiography* by Russell Freedman, winner of the 1988 Newbery Medal.

WALT WHITMAN: One of America's greatest and most innovative poets, Whitman began his epic book of free verse, *Leaves of Grass*, at the age of thirty-six. He continued writing and rewriting the volume his entire life, ending with the 99th edition, published in 1892, the year of his death. His words and wisdom celebrate individual freedom and the dignity of all people everywhere. In time, *Leaves of Grass* proved to be the single most influential volume of poetry in American literary history.

HARRIET TUBMAN: Born a slave in Bucktown, Maryland, Tubman risked her life as a conductor on the Underground Railroad, helping hundreds of slaves out of bondage to freedom. The symbol of strength and bravery, she became known as "The Moses of Her People." In 1978, a United States postage stamp designed by the award-winning children's book illustrator Jerry Pinkney was issued to commemorate her place in American history.

THOMAS ALVA EDISON: An early passion for reading and uncanny curiosity led to Edison's first major invention when he was twenty-one years old—a stock ticker for printing stock exchange operations. During his lifetime he received over one-thousand patents for such devices as the phonograph, moving-picture machines, and the light bulb. In 1867, he established the world's first industrial research laboratories in Menlo Park, New Jersey. Edison's hard work, persistence, and ingenuity revolutionized daily life throughout the world.

ANNE SULLIVAN MACY/HELEN ADAMS KELLER: A serious childhood illness destroyed Keller's sight and hearing. When Sullivan entered her life she awakened new worlds for Keller, teaching her to speak and use sign language. Keller went on to graduate with honors from Radcliffe College, and became a writer and noted lecturer. Keller's incredible and inspirational accomplishments are told in *The Story of My Life* and depicted in the play and film *The Miracle Worker*.

ELEANOR ROOSEVELT: Recognized as one of the most influential women of her time, Roosevelt became known as "First Lady of the World" after her husband, Franklin Delano Roosevelt, the revered president of the United States, died in office. Among her many political accomplishments were her efforts to guarantee minority rights, initiate social programs to enhance the lives of disadvantaged Americans, and help to create the United Nations' Universal Declaration of Human Rights, a crucial document of the twentieth century. An inspiring portrait of this outstanding humanitarian appears in *Eleanor Roosevelt: A Life of Discovery* by Russell Freedman, a 1994 Newbery Honor Book.

GEORGE HERMAN "BABE" RUTH: From the time he was seven until he was twenty years old, Ruth lived in an orphanage. It was there he developed a lifelong interest in baseball. After joining the New York Yankees in 1920, he became an American sports legend. Yankee Stadium, built in 1923 in New York City, is known as "The House That Ruth Built." Cherished by fans throughout the world, he appeared in several silent Hollywood movies and portrayed himself in the award-winning film *Pride of the Yankees*.

LANGSTON HUGHES: Enduring a painful, lonely childhood, moving from relative to relative, Hughes published his first poem, "The Negro Speaks of Rivers," in 1919. His insightful writings dealing with the hopes, sorrows, and dreams of African Americans earned him the title "The Poet of His People." His work continues to be read and loved throughout the world. His only book of poems for young readers, *The Dream Keeper and Other Poems*, has been in print for over six decades. *Free to Dream: The Making of a Poet: Langston Hughes* by Audrey Osofsky relates the life of one of American's most famous contemporary authors.

ROSA LEE PARKS: Parks changed the course of American history when she refused to surrender a seat to a white passenger on a bus in Montgomery, Alabama. Her arrest sparked a 381-day bus boycott led by Martin Luther King, Jr., and resulted in outlawing segregation on public buses. Known as "Mother of the Modern Day Civil Rights Movement," she relates events of her courageous life in *Rosa Parks: My Story* and in *Dear Mrs. Parks: A Dialogue with Today's Youth*.

JOHN FITZGERALD KENNEDY: America's thirty-fifth president was the youngest man and the first Roman Catholic ever elected; he was also the youngest to die in office. During World War II he was nearly killed when a Japanese destroyer rammed his gunboat, PT-109. Surviving the crash he was awarded a medal for bravery for saving his crew. He was assassinated in Dallas, Texas, on November 22, 1963. His 1957 book, *Profiles in Courage*, received the Pulitzer Prize.

MARTIN LUTHER KING, JR: In 1955, when King was pastor at the Dexter Avenue Baptist Church in Montgomery, Alabama, Rosa Lee Parks was arrested for refusing to move to the back of a bus. A support group to defend her chose King as their spokesperson. Soon after, his tireless work on behalf of disadvantaged people became known throughout the world. On August 28, 1963, in Washington, D.C., he delivered his powerful, now-classic "I Have a Dream" speech to over 250,000 people who marched on Washington to protest racial injustice. The speech appears in *I Have a Dream*, featuring paintings by fifteen Coretta Scott King Award and Honor Book artists. On April 4, 1968, he was assassinated in Memphis, Tennessee.

NEIL ALDEN ARMSTRONG and EDWIN EUGENE "BUZZ" ALDRIN, JR. One of the most dramatic moments in history took place on July 20, 1969, when Armstrong set foot on the moon's surface. Nineteen minutes later Aldrin joined him outside the landing craft, together bringing the world one of humankind's greatest adventures. For two hours and fourteen minutes the team explored the moon's landscape, performed experiments, and collected moon rocks. They also planted an American flag on the surface of the moon as a symbol of this incredible feat.

ACKNOWLEDGMENTS

Thanks are due to the following for works reprinted herein:

David Bouchard for "Walt Whitman."
Used by permission of the author, who controls all rights.

Curtis Brown, Ltd. for "Eleanor Roosevelt" by Rebecca Kai Dotlich.
Copyright © 1999 by Rebecca Kai Dotlich; "JFK: Perseverance
Furthers" by Nikki Grimes. Copyright © 1999 by Nikki Grimes;
"Dreamer" by Lee Bennett Hopkins. Copyright © 1999 by Lee
Bennett Hopkins; "A Song for Sacagawea: Lewis and Clark
Expedition—1803–1806" by Jane Yolen. Copyright © 1999 by
Jane Yolen. All reprinted by permission of Curtis Brown, Ltd.

Lee Bennett Hopkins for "Till" by Tom Robert Shields.
Used by permission of Lee Bennett Hopkins for the author.

J. Patrick Lewis for "First Men on the Moon" and
"The Many and the Few."
Used by permission of the author, who controls all rights.

Beverly McLoughland for "The Whippoorwill Calls."
Used by permission of the author, who controls all rights.

Louis Phillips for "When Babe Ruth Hit His Last Home Run."
Used by permission of the author, who controls all rights.

Alice Schertle for "Abe."
Used by permission of the author, who controls all rights.

Lawrence Schimel for "American Wizard" and "This Bell Rings for
Liberty." Used by permission of the author, who controls all rights.

Simon & Schuster for "Martin Luther King Day" from *The Kite That
Braved Old Orchard Beach* by X. J. Kennedy. Text Copyright © 1991
by X. J. Kennedy. Reprinted with the permission of Margaret K.
McElderry Books, an imprint of Simon & Schuster Children's
Publishing Division.